SINGING WHEELS AND
CIRCUS WAGONS

Also Author of
Those Amazing Ringlings and Their Circus
Merle Evans, Maestro of the Circus
Gargantua, Circus Star of the Century

SINGING WHEELS
AND
CIRCUS WAGONS

By
GENE PLOWDEN

The CAXTON PRINTERS, Ltd.
Caldwell, Idaho
1977

International Standard Book Number 0-87004-256-4

Library of Congress Catalog Card Number 75-21135

Lithographed and Bound in the United States of America by
The Caxton Printers, Ltd.
Caldwell, Idaho 83605
126538

CONTENTS

ACKNOWLEDGEMENTS

WRITING A BOOK such as this involves a tremendous amount of research, but it has been a pleasure to work with so many people, particularly the generous and cooperative circus fans.

I especially wish to thank John H. Hurdle, curator of the Ringling Museum of the Circus and former president of the Circus Fans of America, who read the manuscript and offered valuable suggestions.

Also to the following, who offered helpful information or pictures or both:

Gene Christian, Bradenton, Florida; Albert Conover, Xenia, Ohio; Freddie and Bettie Daw, Coral Gables, Florida; Merle and Nena Evans, Sarasota, Florida; Charles S. Meltzer, Philadelphia, Pennsylvania; Lloyd Morgan and Colonel W. W. Naramore, Sarasota, Florida.

Fred Pfening, Jr., Columbus, Ohio; Orlo J. Rahn, Davenport, Iowa; Earl and Betty Schmid, Pittsburg, Pennsylvania; Arthur C. Spellman, West Palm Beach, Florida; Russell and Mildred Warner, Harrisburg, Pennsylvania; Robert F. Wigglesworth, Bettendorf, Iowa; and Dr. Gilbert Williams, Fort Lauderdale, Florida.

GENE PLOWDEN

INTRODUCTION

A NOSTALGIC LOOK at the grand old circus parades, now gone from the American scene for many, many years, never to return.

And a glimpse of some of the gorgeous parade wagons and band chariots with their fine wood carvings, teams of up to forty horses that pulled them, and the singing wheels they moved on!

Here is a book to delight the eye, quicken the pulse, and bring back memories of "the good old days."

— G. P.

SINGING WHEELS AND
CIRCUS WAGONS

CHAPTER ONE

HERE IT COMES!

IF YOU'VE NEVER STOOD on a sidewalk or looked out a window and watched a circus parade go by, you have missed one of the most memorable experiences mankind ever was privileged to enjoy.

These thrilling pageantries have been gone from the American scene for nearly half a century now, and more's the pity, for they can never return.

Just as man cannot duplicate the beauty of a rainbow, so he can never re-create the setting for these spine-tingling spectacles. He may blast a human being to the moon and bring him home again, but he cannot bring back the circus parade, any more than he can stop the passing of time or mend a broken heart.

Circus parades offered every color, sound, sight, and smell one could dream of — a living river of beauty and pageantry, flowing to the rhythm of great brass bands, the shuffling of elephants, and ring of horse's hooves on cobblestones and concrete.

And the songs of wagon wheels!

Man has loved parades, and benefited from them, for centuries. Royalty and nobility rode in ceremonial processions to impress their subjects and perhaps to get a breath of fresh air outside their musty old palaces and castles.

Military leaders insisted upon displays of marching men and weapons of war to stimulate patriotic fervor, warn possible enemies, and draw liberal allotments from the public treasury.

Parades have been used effectively to celebrate historic dates and religious holidays, to promote fairs and festivals, and to stir up interest in athletic contests and political campaigns.

But none could compare with the grand old circus parade, surely the most powerful advertising medium ever devised. In fact, it was the only method our earliest traveling entertainment enterprises had of telling the people "The circus is in town!"

In colonial times, and even until early in the twentieth century, the parade was a most effective means of announcing the circus's arrival. It gave the populace a tantalizing glimpse of some of the many thrills and wonders featured in the performances, and it cost nothing but a little time and effort.

Small circuses, called "mud shows" because heavy rains quickly turned dirt roads and wagon trails into quagmires, had no other advertising media except perhaps a few window cards and handbills.

They'd stop the caravan at a convenient creek or under a clump of trees on the edge of town to freshen up after what likely had been a long and tiring journey from the last stand.

Here they would wash the mud or dust off

First sight of the circus usually was the owner or manager riding in a buggy or surrey.

Mounted bands were featured on many circus parades. This one was in the Ringling Bros. Circus in 1909.

horses and wagons, clean themselves and don costumes, then ride into town behind a mounted trumpeter accompanied by one or more horsemen holding banners and shouting, "Hold your horses! The circus is coming!"

The parade was held near noon when streets were filled with people. The procession would move down the main street past the courthouse or town hall with band blaring, clowns cavorting, and everyone smiling and bowing and waving on the way to the circus grounds. It was an invitation to join them, and it was irresistible.

Horses and elephants were fitted with heavy leather harness to withstand wear, decorated with huge brass medallions, and with plumes atop bridles and hames. On the road, elephants often wore leather or canvas boots to protect their feet from stones.

As circuses grew larger and many traveled by rail, parades became elaborate productions, an indication of the show's magnitude as well as its diversity — horses, elephants, camels, and snarling wild animals; cages, wagons, chariots, tableaux; several bands, and hundreds of men, women, and children mounted or walking.

Every detail was carefully planned, and the parade moved with military precision. This was necessary because the route was through the heart of the city, and a parade sometimes stretched for one or even two miles.

Competition was fierce, and rival owners often spent lavish sums for great bandwagons, tableau wagons, chariots, and floats. Band

Parades always were great attractions. This was the Young Buffalo Wild West Shows in 1912.

Gollmar Bros. displayed this elephant herd in the 1893 parade.

members wore colorful uniforms, and all performers were dressed in gorgeous costumes.

The larger circuses usually had not only a
main band of perhaps thirty or more musicians,
but a sideshow band and ticket seller's band —
maybe a clown band and even a children's band.
Music was the lifeblood of the circus, brassy and
loud.

Outdoor entertainment ventures had to over-
come many prejudices and obstacles. For example, cities and towns slapped them with heavy
license fees and taxes; merchants complained
they hurt business; and an editor once com-
mented in his newspaper that "the circus took
enough money out of town to pay for three fine
lectures."

*Texas Longhorns were featured on the Young Buffalo Wild West
Shows in 1912.*

Wagons of many types and sizes were seen in parades. This is Fred K. Leonard on the Bailey Bros. Circus in 1905.

Sheriffs and police chiefs, as well as other city officials, sometimes demanded blocks of tickets. Once the governor of Louisiana threatened to have every animal on the show dipped in vats of disinfectant if Ringling Bros. and Barnum & Bailey Circus gave a scheduled performance at the same time his favorite college football team was playing in another part of town.

Circus men and women met trials, tribulations, and frustrations with fortitude, ingenuity, and hard work. They made their way in the world without help from local, state, or national governments. Always on their own, they provided clean, wholesome entertainment for all the family and never needed a censor.

When asphalt paving came into general use, the circus faced an unexpected barrier. Iron rims on heavy wagon wheels cut into the pavement and had to be replaced with rubber tires.

Michievous boys sometimes had a field day of fun even before the circus made its way to the lot. If the show arrived before dawn, lanterns were placed on strategic corners to mark the route from railroad station to the grounds.

"We liked to move those lanterns around," a gray-haired circus fan recently recalled. "Pretty soon the circus would be scattered all over town!"

At other times cardboard arrows were tacked on telegraph poles to point the way. Turning these in the opposite direction would create utter confusion and send the circus far off its intended route.

Circuses tried not to play the same city on the same day, or even in the same general area, but this happened occasionally. In 1892, the Barnum & Bailey Circus and George W. Hall & Sons United Shows played Chicago on the same day and only a few blocks apart. The Barnum & Bailey parade left the lot just as the Hall procession reached it; they marched in competition for several blocks.

And in 1906, also in Chicago — a favorite city for circuses — the Carl Hagenbeck parade went north on Cottage Grove Avenue while Gentry Bros. Circus marched in the other direction on the opposite side of the street.

In their glory days, circuses would arrive in town before dawn aboard two, three, or even four railroad trains, the long, gleaming cars packed with animals, cages, wagons, and equipment and swarming with workmen.

What a thrill it was to roll out of bed in the dark and hurry down to the station to see the trains come in, to watch them unload tons and tons of trappings, see the elephants and horses pull the great wagons and dens from the flats, and see an empty lot transformed as if by magic into a canvas city of living wonders from all over the world.

It was even more exciting to watch the parade move down the main street. It might cover as many as five or even ten miles, depending upon the distance from the circus lot to downtown, but it went on, rain or shine, and it was beautiful to behold.

The parade "call" was blown twenty minutes before the procession was to move off; everyone in personnel was involved, and each was on his or

Four horses pulled this elaborately carved Pawnee Bill wagon in 1905.

her best behavior, under strict rules of conduct laid down by management. These specified what clothing must be worn, and how. There would be no smoking, spitting, or chewing. Drivers must be clean-shaven and their boots blackened; none must appear in shirt sleeves or with vests unbuttoned. Ladies must wear gauntlet gloves in the parade and in the grand entry.

Riders and drivers must sit straight, keep horses' heads up, and move no faster than a walk unless otherwise ordered. All units were to keep thirty feet apart except the mounted band, which must keep together and play continuously.

Riders carrying banners and flags moved ahead, followed by the owner or manager in top hat or straw skimmer, depending upon the weather. He rode in a shiny surrey or buggy with the top down, drawn by matched horses or ponies.

Buglers and trumpeters were followed by the great bandwagon crammed with musicians, drawn by six, ten, or even forty horses. Then came cages, tableau wagons and a band; ladies in glittering costumes riding horses of similar color and size; floats, more cages, tableaux; more ladies on horseback, a band, men riding high-stepping steeds or driving teams of great draft horses.

The show might also have a Wild West section, complete with cowboys and Indians and its own brass band. There might be Cossacks in full regalia, a mounted band, assorted animals, birds, and reptiles, then twenty or thirty

The great Two Hemispheres bandwagon was drawn by 40 horses in the Barnum & Bailey parades, this one in 1903.

Outriders kept the parade units in line. This was in the Ringling Bros. Circus in 1915.

elephants, swinging and swaying along, trunk to tail.

Finally came the calliope, belching smoke and steam, its whistles whining and wailing, drawn by six or eight horses. The circus claimed this musical monster could be heard ten miles away, "yet its tones are as softly sweet as a lover's lute." Indeed, it seemed to be.

The parade was far more realistic and appealing than motion pictures, even with sound and color — more than radio or television, which came along many years later.

It had all those tantalizing sounds of horses' hooves ringing on pavement, elephants shuffling their stubby legs, harness and trappings clicking and clanking, wagon wheels whining and creaking against axle shafts and brake shoes, drivers clucking and talking to their horses, elephants, camels, and zebras as they hurried along.

And sprinkled through it all were clowns in their funny costumes and makeup — dancing and tumbling, waving and whistling every step of the way.

It was weird, intoxicating, and blood-stirring. It had living, moving color, and it had enough sights, sounds, and smells to kindle the fires of imagination and quicken the pulse of every man, woman, and child along the line of march and draw them to the ticket wagons like ants to picnics.

Crowds from the sidewalks and stores fell in behind the calliope and followed it to the circus grounds, where there was time to eat popcorn, drink lemonade, see the sideshow, or visit the

Some circus parades had clown bands. This wagon was drawn by six white horses.

menagerie and whiff the pungent odors there before the performance began.

The parades were inspiring, memorable spectacles, overpowering in their appeal and enchanting to all because they offered such a vast variety of things to see, to savor, and remember. And they were "absolutely free!"

Americans saw and delighted in circus parades for one hundred happy years, from the 1830s to the 1930s. Then motor vehicles began to clog the streets and avenues of every city in the land; there was no place left to ride or walk, to move people, wagons, and animals.

And so these great processions drifted into history, to become only vivid peaks in yon misty mountains of memories.

*This 16-pony train pulled an ornate wagon in Barnum & Bailey
parades in 1883-85.*

CHAPTER TWO

THE EARLIEST WAGONS

IN THE CRADLE DAYS of the Republic, circus troupes performed in buildings in such cities as New York, Philadelphia, Baltimore, Washington, Charleston, and Savannah, as well as on lots adjoining hotels and livery stables and on other suitable grounds.

Among the first to go under canvas was the Quick & Mead Circus, with a fifty-foot spread; Howes & Turner, who boasted "a full top canvas"; and Buckley & Weeks, with a tent twenty-five feet in diameter which they claimed could seat 800 patrons.

This was about the time (1823) that the Chatham Garden in New York City advertised "a complete pavilion theatre covered with a broad expanse of white canvas which will protect the audience from the evening dews."

The few paved, planked, or corduroy roads that roamed through eastern cities and towns were generally connected with muddy or dusty country trails, which encouraged circuses to travel by water and rail. This they did, touring on the Great Lakes, the Ohio, Missouri, and Mississippi rivers, and even out into the Gulf of Mexico from New Orleans to Mobile and Pensacola.

Among these were Spalding & Rogers Circus on the Floating Palace, the James Raymond, and the Banjo; Dan Rice on the Alleghany Mail; and the Olympic Circus Company.

It is interesting to note that the first circus to travel by rail did so in December 1838, when a troupe headed by Charles Bacon and Edwin Derious made a trip over the new line built by Central Railroad and Banking Company of Georgia between Macon and Forsyth, a distance of approximately twenty-five miles.

With this circus was young John Robinson, who with his son and later his grandson operated popular outdoor entertainment ventures, mostly

Columbia bandwagon shown in Barnum & Bailey parade about 1912.

throughout the South, until 1916. Even after that the name lived on, and the last John Robinson Circus, then owned by the Ringlings, left the scene following the 1930 season.

In a newspaper advertisement in 1835, Macomber, Welch & Co.'s New England Zoological Exhibition announced that "the band will be drawn in a splendid music carriage," perhaps the first appearance of a circus bandwagon on the American horizon.

Franconi's Colossal Hippodrome entered the city of Hartford, Connecticut, in 1846 in a parade reportedly highlighted by a band "playing in a chariot drawn by ten matched horses."

Chariots and fairy tale floats were featured in many parades.

As a chariot it couldn't have been much by later standards, when bandwagons measured twenty feet or more in length and were elaborately decorated with intricate wood carvings and quantities of paint and gold leaf.

Earliest circuses used bandwagons that resembled family sleighs mounted on large wheels, the sides painted in bright colors. They were drawn by two, four, or eight horses, depending upon the show's available power.

All early cage wagons and chariots were of light construction, with large, carriage-like wheels. It wasn't until the 1870's, when railroads began to span the country, that circuses generally took to rails and began featuring costly and enormous parade wagons.

There also were cage wagons, baggage wagons, advertising wagons, and even ticket wagons painted and lettered in gaudy colors, though in earlier times all bore the name of the circus and little else.

Forerunner of the bandwagon may have been the "Apollonicon," which appeared about 1851 on the Spalding & Rogers Circus. Named for Apollo, Greek god of the sun, prophecy, music, medicine, and poetry, it included organ pipes, cymbals, drums, whistles, bells, horns, and gongs played mechanically. What a racket it must have made!

When Spalding & Rogers appeared in Hartford, Connecticut, in 1854, the circus parade was said to have been led by "a grand floral car drawn by forty horses."

The following season this circus featured what it called "the massive ornamented music

Larger circuses also had colored bands. This one paraded in a shell type bandwagon.

The calliope came at the end of the parade. And there it goes!

car called the Apollonicon, drawn by forty horses hitched four abreast." Howes & Cushing also had an apollonicon when it toured the British Isles in the late 1850s.

Some authorities credit William Hoyt of Dupont, Indiana, with the idea of producing music through a set of steam whistles about 1851, but it was not until 1855 that Joshua C. Stoddard of Worcester, Massachusetts, obtained a patent on "a new musical instrument to be played by the agency of steam or highly compressed air."

Stoddard received more than a dozen other patents, but the calliope appears to have been his most prominent and lasting invention. It came on the scene just in time to whine its way into the hearts of America through the circus parade.

One of the few musical instruments to have originated in this country, the first calliope had only eight keys and as many pitched pipes. Steam came from a coal- or wood-burning boiler, and pressure on the keys opened valves that let steam into the pipes.

Stoddard organized the American Steam Music Company, put his calliope on a flat car, and serenaded towns along the line. He reasoned that the calliope might replace church bells, but congregations wanted no part of it, and its first commercial appearance was on a Hudson River steamer.

The earliest calliopes (ka-li-o-pea to towners but kal-ley-ope to circus folk) included a fingerboard to operate the whistle valves, a pin drum for depressing the keys, a player's seat, and a steam traction engine whose boiler supplied the steam.

The player had to be a brave soul, for he was sprayed with sparks, sprinkled with steam, and blistered by the hot keys. Some photographs of the time show husky attendants to look after the boilers.

Circus owners were quick to see the value of this novel music-maker because no one could miss the loud, penetrating tones that came from the steaming, smoking contraption as it whistled and whined its way to the show grounds. Naturally, it was placed at the very end of the street parade, to provide a fitting climax.

Within a few years after Stoddard received his patent, most circuses of any size had a calliope of twenty-one or thirty-two whistles made of brass or copper, the whole operation mounted on one wagon or two. The wagons were heavily carved and gilded, and the circus that couldn't afford a calliope just wasn't "with it." P. T. Barnum boasted that his calliope was made with silver whistles.

In the book *Merle Evans, Maestro of the Circus* (Seemann, 1971), the man who led the Ringling Bros. and Barnum & Bailey Circus band for fifty years had this to say about the calliope:

"These were actually a variation of the organ or piano. We jokingly called them 'steam fiddles' or 'steam pianos.' Our old steam calliope weighed around seven thousand pounds. It had a boiler but ran out of steam quite often, so they'd have to fire up and make more steam.

"The calliope has no range, but, Christ, you can hear one for miles. The one we had on the old

Cotton Blossom showboat was hooked up to the boiler, so we had plenty of steam. You could hear it five or maybe ten miles up and down the Mississippi and out into the swamps.

"I always liked the calliope but never learned to play one very well. They got out of tune in wet weather, but they never missed drawing the crowds. There aren't too many of them around any more, except in museums."

The Civil War put a serious crimp in circus operations, especially in the South, where most of the fighting took place. Travel there was severely restricted, and most inhabitants were too busy or too broke to think of outside entertainment.

Yankee Robinson, whose real name was Fayette Lodawick Robinson, had to leave one of the Carolinas — some say Charleston and some say Raleigh — in a hurry because of his nickname.

Dan Rice, one of the premier circus operators of his time, opened the 1861 season in Washington, D.C., but soon departed for safer territory, touring towns along the Ohio River. Spalding & Rogers tied up the Floating Palace at New Albany, Indiana, and went to South America.

The Robinson & Lake Circus was forced to flee Lexington, Kentucky, and operate north of the Ohio during the conflict, and Howes & Norton was trapped in Nashville, Tennessee, for six weeks in 1864, caught between the lines of Union and Confederate troops.

Some circuses continued to operate in New York state, along the Ohio and upper Mississippi

The Five Graces bandwagon seen in Berlin, Germany May 14, 1900. It was drawn by 40 horses, with Jake Posey on the box.

For several years the Five Graces bandwagon was at winter quarters in Brideport, Conn. (J. T. McCaddon Papers, Princeton Univ. Library)

rivers, and on the West Coast. But the South, always a happy hunting ground for entertainers, lay beaten and barren for fifteen years after the first shots were fired at Fort Sumter in April 1861, and circuses generally avoided it.

The record reflects that during the period of 1861-65 only twenty-six circuses were active in America, compared with the years 1926-30, for example, when fifty-three were on the road. In both instances many lasted only one season or less, indicating the high mortality rate in the outdoor amusement business.

CHAPTER THREE

A LOOK AT THE PAST

WHEN THE CIVIL WAR ended, the whole country began to grow, and circuses with it. Many of them went on rails, although this often meant extra hours of back-breaking work because lines were built with different gauges. But circus folk never were allergic to work.

Wheels had to be adjusted to axles, car bodies transferred from one set of wheels to another, or entire loads moved from one set of cars and flats to another.

Spalding & Rogers had a railroad circus, and so did Dan Castello, who had come out of Racine, Wisconsin, and was the first to make a coast-to-coast tour with circus and menagerie in 1869.

A number of circuses appeared on the scene in the 1870s, best known being P. T. Barnum and partners, which began with an agreement made in October 1870 with Castello and William Cameron Coup of Delavan, Wisconsin.

Coup and Castello were partners in a circus that year called Dan Castello's Circus, but Coup wanted to expand by joining with Barnum, the promoter, lecturer, and museum proprietor, who could supply capital and prestige. Coup became manager and stayed with Barnum through the

1875 season. Castello was producer, and S. H. Hurd, Barnum's son-in-law, was treasurer.

By this time Barnum had published a newspaper, served a jail term for libel, operated museums in New York and Philadelphia, toured with Aaron Turner's traveling circus company, exhibited General Tom Thumb, lectured, arranged a tour with Jenny Lind, traveled widely in this country and abroad, and retired to his home, Waldemere, at Bridgeport, Connecticut. He called himeself "the public's obedient servant."

The enterprise was billed as P. T. Barnum's Museum, Menagerie and Circus, and it traveled by wagon through New York and New England during the 1871 season.

Coup arranged with railroads to operate excursion trains at reduced fares. This, coupled with an intensive advertising and promotion campaign in newspapers and with posters, brought people from all directions.

Barnum, ever the promoter, claimed credit for the bonanza of business, but he spent little time with the show. He up-dated his autobiography, "Struggles and Triumphs," every few years, and in the 1873 edition he boasted:

"In sending these last pages to the printer in March 1872 I may say that my manager, Mr. Coup, his assistants, and myself have been busy since New Year's in reorganizing our great traveling show, building new wagons and cages, and painting, gilding, and repairing the others.

"One of the great carved, mirrored, and gilded chariots, from England, used by me in 1871, is a

*The Five Graces appeared in this Hagenbeck-Wallace parade at
Decatur, Ill., May 16, 1934.*

grand affair, made telescopic, and when extended to its full height reaches an altitude of forty feet, on top of which, in our street processions, we place a young lady costumed to impersonate the Goddess of Liberty."

Concluding his account of the "great carved, mirrored, and gilded chariot," Barnum wrote that gilding this one vehicle cost him "about five thousand dollars — enough to build a nice house in the country."

The show opened in Brooklyn on April 10, 1871, under what it claimed was the largest area of canvas spread for a circus up to that time. It had waxworks, dioramas, Swiss bell ringers, the Cardiff Giant, Admiral Dot, Colonel Goshen, a family of Fiji "cannibals," and a giraffe.

Coup wanted to put the circus on rails, but Barnum was against it. He was never particularly fond of railroads and claimed they never liked him because while he was a member of the Connecticut Legislature in 1867 he pushed through a bill regulating commuter fares on the New York and New Haven Railroad.

Coup argued that the show was too large to move by wagon and that they must put it on rails or reduce it. Barnum finally agreed and quickly claimed credit for the success of "P. T. Barnum's Great Traveling Exposition and World's Fair."

In the 1872 season it was "P. T. Barnum's Great Traveling World's Fair consisting of Museum, Menagerie, Caravan, Hippodrome, Gallery of Statuary and Fine Arts, Polytechnic Institute, Zoological Garden, and 100,000 curiosities, combined with Dan Castello's, Sig.

Steel rims cut into asphalt paving, So rubber tires were substituted. Here the Five Graces moves on dual rubber wheels.

Sebastian's and Mr. D'Atelie's Grand Triple Equestrian and Hippodromatic Exposition."

Coup and Barnum parted company at the end of the 1875 season, and the old promotional genius went in with a group known as the Flatfoots. This was an association of show owners, managers, and investors, many of whom lived in upper New York state, who reportedly organized to monopolize the territory.

Beginning in 1835 the Flatfoots were prominent in circuses and menageries until about 1873, when James A. Bailey and James E. Cooper joined forces to organize the Cooper & Bailey Circus. It went on rails in 1876, spent two years touring Australia, New Zealand, and South America, then came home to figure prominently in this country's amusement business.

When Coup left him, Barnum's show combined with one owned by the Flatfoots, operating under the Barnum title through 1880. The merger was effected by putting both shows up for sale at auction and allowing the Flatfoots to bid in what equipment they wanted.

Meanwhile Cooper & Bailey bought Howes' Great London Circus and Sanger's Royal British Menagerie, combining these with their own and operating through the 1879 and 1880 seasons as Howes' Great London Circus, Sanger's Royal British Menagerie, and Cooper & Bailey's International Allied Shows.

Bailey and James L. Hutchinson bought out the Flatfoots prior to the 1881 season and went into partnership with Barnum as P. T. Barnum's Greatest Show on Earth, Howes' Great London Circus, and Sanger's Royal British Menagerie.

Bailey and Barnum did not always agree, and Bailey sold out his interest to Cooper and William Washington Cole after that season. He rejoined the Barnum operation in 1888, when he was given a free hand as manager.

When Adam Forepaugh died in 1890, Cooper and Bailey bought the Adam Forepaugh Circus, and when Cooper died two years later, Bailey acquired his share of the partnership.

Barnum's death on April 7, 1891, did not affect the Barnum & Bailey Circus, which came to life when Bailey bought out Cooper, Cole, and Hutchinson.

The Barnum & Bailey Circus grew rapidly in the last decade of the century under Bailey's capable management, but it had considerable competition from the Ringling Bros., Gollmar Bros., Mighty Haag, and others.

Toughest of all came from the five Ringling brothers — Al, Alf T., Otto, Charles, and John — who started a "hall show" in 1882 and, in cooperation with Yankee Robinson, put on their first circus performance in their hometown of Baraboo, Wisconsin, on May 19, 1884.

The Ringling Bros. Circus leased the Van Amburgh title in 1889 and a year later put their show on rails. By the end of the century they had become a formidable power in the circus field.

Bailey acquired an interest in the Sells Bros. Circus and merged this with the Great Adam Forepaugh Show. He also controlled the Buffalo Bill Wild West Show, and in 1896 his three circuses competed with the Ringlings at no less than forty-five stands. Bailey took his Barnum & Bailey Circus to Europe in 1897 and did not come home until November 1902.

In his authoritative work, *A History of the Circus in America* (Caxton, 1959), the late George L. Chindahl observed:

"During the closing decades of the nineteenth century and the first two decades of the twentieth, the American circus attained its prime in the number, size, and quality of the organizations catering to the public, and in the development of diverse forms, such as the Wild West Show, the dog and pony show, the trained wild animal show, the one-, two-, or three-car railroad show, and the indoor circus."

There have been numerous "brothers" in the business, some real and some fictional. Related ones include the Ringlings, Sells, Gollmar, Jones, Miller, Mills, and others, the latest being the Feld brothers, Irvin and Israel, of Ringling-Barnum fame.

There also were some family circuses, among them Orton, Whitney, Wixom, and the Cristianis. Two of the best known were operated by women. The Mollie Bailey show, founded by Gus Bailey around 1879 and run by him until his death in 1896, was taken over by his widow, who, with her children, operated it successfully until she died in 1918. Rose Kilian and her children had a mule-drawn family circus for about twenty years, commencing in 1904. Its territory was the South, and it was billed as "the old reliable Southern Exhibition."

Bailey made a gallant effort to overshadow the Ringlings in the 1903 season. He expanded the Barnum & Bailey Circus to ninety cars, against sixty-three for the Ringlings, and he staged one of the largest and most magnificent circus parades ever seen in America.

However, by the end of the season Bailey realized, as did the Ringlings, that competition was hurting both, so they agreed to divide territory. The next year Bailey sold the Ringlings half interest in the Forepaugh-Sells Circus and turned over its management to them.

James A. Bailey died on April 11, 1906, while readying the Barnum & Bailey Circus for the season, and George O. Starr became manager of Barnum & Bailey, Ltd. corporation. At the season's end, W. W. Cole and J. T. McCaddon were named to the board of directors. Cole became

When the Five Graces was restored, it went to the Ringling Museum of the Circus. Here are Ken Donahue and Mel Miller, Museum director.

manager of the Barnum & Bailey Circus and Buffalo Bill Wild West Show.

The 1906 season was a bad one for Barnum & Bailey, mainly because of torrential rains in the Midwest and a costly blowdown at Iowa City, Iowa. A financial depression was on, too, and stockholders agreed to sell the grand old circus to the Ringlings for $410,000.

The five brothers from Baraboo now controlled three circuses — Ringling Bros., Barnum & Bailey, and Forepaugh-Sells. In the transaction Colonel William F. Cody (Buffalo Bill) regained control of the Wild West show bearing his name, which the Ringlings claimed they never wanted anyway.

The money panic over, circuses began to grow, and in 1910 Barnum & Bailey and Ringling Bros. each traveled aboard eighty-four railroad cars. Eight other circuses and Wild West shows were aboard twenty-four or more cars that season, with some twenty-five smaller ones on the road.

The outdoor entertainment dollar was being split so many ways that Charles Ringling proposed circus men do something about competition. Accordingly, representatives of ten circuses met in Chicago in December 1910 and agreed to certain rules of behavior.

At the meeting were men from Ringling Bros., Barnum & Bailey, Forepaugh-Sells, Hagenbeck-Wallace, John Robinson, Gentry Bros., Mighty Haag, Sells-Floto, Sun Bros., and Buffalo Bill-Pawnee Bill Wild West.

They posted bonds of performance, opening

membership rolls to all circuses and Wild West shows. However, the association didn't last out the season, and competition continued as bitter as ever.

In the years between 1900 and 1920, about 170 circuses and Wild West shows toured the country, some lasting a season or less. Consolidations were in order; motorized and indoor circuses blossomed.

There was considerable mechanization — trucks, tractors, power stake-drivers, spool wagons for canvas. Electric lights replaced gas, and in some instances electric fans were installed.

The Ringlings operated their two big circuses as separate units through the 1918 season, when World War I shortages, mounting costs, and high taxes made consolidation compulsory. So they abandoned their winter quarters at Baraboo and moved in with Barnum & Bailey at Bridgeport, Connecticut. There the two properties were merged, and on March 29, 1919, the first performance of Ringling Bros. and Barnum & Bailey Combined Circus took place in New York's Madison Square Garden.

Charles Ringling died in December 1926, leaving John the sole surviving brother — circus king by reputation as well as physical dimensions, and best known member of the clan.

In 1927 he moved winter quarters from Bridgeport to Sarasota on Florida's Gulf Coast, built a mansion and an art museum there, bought a hotel and started construction on another, drilled for oil, opened a bank, and promoted an island subdivision.

For John Ringling, the year 1929 was one misfortune after another. His good friend, promoter George L. (Tex) Rickard, died in January; his wife, Mable Burton Ringling, passed away in June; and financial storms began to form.

Jerry Mugivan and Bert Bowers, experienced showmen, now held ownership of Hagenbeck-Wallace, Howes' Great London, John Robinson, and Sparks circuses. With Ed Ballard joining them, they acquired Sells-Floto and Yankee Robinson, formed the American Circus Corporation, and added the Al G. Barnes show.

They proposed to combine Sells-Floto and Hagenbeck-Wallace into one big show and open the 1930 season in Madison Square Garden, which John Ringling considered his bailiwick. He was board chairman when that edition of the Garden opened in 1925, and he wasn't about to give up that lucrative spot to a rival.

It was either that or buy the American Circus Corporation — which he did for two million dollars, $450,000 of it in cash. Now, in addition to his own mammoth circus, he owned Al G. Barnes, Hagenbeck-Wallace, Sells-Floto, John Robinson, and Sparks, plus titles to Buffalo Bill, Gollmar Bros., Howes' Great London, and Yankee Robinson.

Six weeks after the deal the stock market crashed, a paralyzing depression began, and money to be spent for entertainment became scarcer month by month.

John Ringling sent out six circuses in 1930 — Ringling Bros. and Barnum & Bailey, Al G. Barnes, Hagenbeck-Wallace, John Robinson,

This was the scene on Nov. 11, 1967, when the Ringling Bros. and Barnum & Bailey Circus ownership changed hands in Rome, Italy (Wide World Photo)

Sells-Floto, and Sparks. Somehow he managed to visit most of them during the losing season that ended by mid-October, dipping into supervision and routing as he always liked to do.

John also went to Europe and there found himself another wife. He and Emily Haag Buck were married by Mayor Frank ("Boss") Hague in Jersey City, New Jersey, on December 19, 1930.

The John Robinson Circus went off the road, Sparks and Sells-Floto were cut down, but 1931 was another unprofitable season as the depression deepened. Sparks never went out again, and 1932 was the last year for Sells-Floto.

John Ringling couldn't meet his notes, and a group of New York financiers took control of his circus empire. Ringling passed away December 2, 1936. John Ringling North, a son of the only sister in the family, gained command the following spring.

North, as capable a circus man as his shrewd old Uncle John, bought a gorilla, billed it as "Gargantua the Great," and thereby saved the circus. Gargantua trouped through twelve seasons and was the circus star of the century, the biggest attraction since Jumbo.

Hagenbeck-Wallace made its final tour in 1935, and Al G. Barnes left the road in 1938. From 1939 through 1943, only Ringling Bros. and Barnum & Bailey and Cole Bros. traveled on rails.

A few other shows appeared after World War II, but by 1956 the Ringling-Barnum combine was the only railroad circus left in America. On July 16 of that year, in Pittsburgh, the big top went down for the last time. What was left of

"The Greatest Show on Earth" was loaded aboard three trains and sent to winter quarters.

The following season it went out in fifteen railroad cars, plus a fleet of trucks, trailers, and automobiles. But there was no big top, no menagerie, no cookhouse or other reminders of old circus days.

Plainly such outdoor entertainment ventures had become vitims of changing tastes and times, of shopping plazas, condominiums, and choking traffic; of radio, television, and sports spectacles.

On November 11, 1967 — Armistice Day then — John Ringling North announced from the Coliseum in Rome that he had sold the grand old Ringling Bros and Barnum & Bailey Combined Circus to the Hoffeld Corporation of Delaware. That was Judge Roy Hofheinz (of Houston, Texas, and Astrodome fame) and the brothers Irvin and Israel Feld of Washington, D.C.

The show has continued its annual tours, playing in auditoriums and convention halls coast to coast. Since 1969 it has gone out in two units, the Red and the Blue. Most animals and equipment still go by train, but many of the people travel in trailers or by automobile.

Early in 1974 the corporation opened "Circus World," a showplace in central Florida.

More than a score of circuses were on the road for the 1974 season, including Clyde Beatty-Cole Bros., largest under canvas, and Hoxie Bros., first to introduce a circular big top in modern times.

At least two-thirds of these were promotion shows, operating with local sponsors who sold tickets and shared in profits. This arrangement usually assures a suitable location and avoids conflict with other entertainment.

And so circuses continue to go to the people, as they have for two hundred years, in cities large and small, in shopping plazas and cross-road hamlets, bringing to children of all ages in all walks of life a taste of what used to be.

So much for circus history. Let's get back to the wagons.

CHAPTER FOUR

GORGEOUS CHARIOTS

THE CIRCUS HAS ALWAYS found business by going after it, and one-day stands are the rule. No other undertaking operates with such mobility and under so many handicaps, which explains in part why running a circus can be as risky as raising orchids outdoors.

There is always the threat of fire, blowdown, wreck, or other disaster; accidents or illness among humans and animals can put it out of business, and a week of bad weather can cripple it severely. It takes long hours of hard work, boundless optimism, dedication, and determination to keep a circus on the road.

In the last 200 years, well over 2,500 circuses have come and gone in the United States. Only one dates back to the last century or even to the last World War.

The golden age of the circus in America grew out of decades of experience, going back to the early days of the nation when horses and wagons brought troupes of performers into town for an "engagement." For fifteen years after the Civil War these increased in size and numbers as the country crept back to normal. Competition grew and bitter rivalries developed; many crisscrossed the country looking for business.

In these glory days, which lasted for fifty years starting about 1880, circuses grew as rapidly as America itself; many prospered. Owners hired the most capable managers and cagey promoters they could find, and they spent lavishly on horses and virtually every type of wild animal available.

To all this they added flats, stockcars, and coaches — great acts, fine brass bands, sturdy wagons, and some of the gaudiest chariots on earth.

Chariots? You bet. For instance, Welch, Delavan & Nathan's National Circus featured in 1848 what it called "The Armamaxa, or Imperial Persian Chariot, drawn by thirty horses."

"This gorgeous chariot, from the manufac-

This elaborately carved ticket wagon was on the Sig. Sautelle Circus in 1900. Photographed at Westerly, R.I.

The B. E. Wallace Circus (1884-1906) featured this shell-type bandwagon.

Barnum & Bailey had this double den cage wagon on the circus in 1909.

tory of J. Stephenson & Co., 27th St., New York, has just been completed," the circus crowed.

"For its graceful proportions, exquisite workmanship, and brilliant emblazonry it has never been equalled either in ancient or modern times. It is said to be fashioned after the model of the Imperial Chariots of Persia, during the reign of Cyrus the Great.

"The sides of the chariot are divided into six panels, separated by richly gilded scrollwork in the style of Louis XIV. The scrollwork is bordered by beautiful frill moulding, and runs along the top as well as the bottom of the chariot.

"The seat of the charioteer is covered with a rich hammercloth of purple velvet trimmed with deep silver fringe, pendant from a border of blue

This bandwagon was on the Mighty Haag Railroad Show in 1912.

Howes. Golden Globe bandwagon, without the top carvings, was used late in the last century. This was called "Hungarians on Parade."

and yellow velvet, the whole decorated with eagles, equestrian figures, stars and flowers, wrought in gold and silver.

"The charioteer appears borne along between the expanded wings of two mighty dragons, apparently of massive gold, which couch above the four wheels of the chariot."

Van Amburgh & Co. Circus had what it called "a colossal golden chariot" during the 1860s. In later years this vehicle appeared on Sells Bros. Circus and with Rhoda-Royal. It was described in these words:

"A magnificent band chariot, one of the finest ever built in America and modeled much in the style of the ancient Roman triumphal chariots, almost entirely covered by elaborate carvings, richly gilded, relieved by several small panels, and decorated with exquisitely executed paintings.

"Lions, tigers, lynxes, wolves, and other animals figure among the ornamental carved work, and the effect of the whole when fully completed and put on the road behind a team of ten superb horses is brilliant and imposing in the extreme."

Owners proudly announced that this particular piece of rolling splendor weighed 6,000 pounds and cost $7,000.

Forty-horse teams were featured by several circuses, commencing perhaps with Spalding &

*This spec float was used on the Ringling Bros. and Barnum &
Bailey Circus about 1930.*

Rogers around 1849-50. Yankee Robinson, Dan Rice, Barnum & Bailey, Ringling Bros., and others used the forty-horse hitch from time to time.

This was a spectacular feature, but it took a real man to guide the mass of horsepower through narrow, winding streets — drivers like Jim Thomas, J. W. Paul, Jake Posey, and others.

Adam Forepaugh, Jr., drove a thirty-nine-horse team on the Forepaugh Circus in the 1890 season, making one trip around the hippodrome track at each performance. This included a lead

Known as the Egypt float, this appeared in the Ringling Bros. and Barnum & Bailey Circus parades in 1930.

horse hitched to a singletree on the end of a two-inch rope attached to the parade wagon.

This was described as having two horses weighing about 2,000 pounds each hitched to the wagon with heavy britchings and neck yokes. Between them and the lead horse were thirty-six others, two abreast, with halters and lines tying them to the larger rope. When they circled the track, men at strategic points prevented them from darting out any exit.

Jake Posey drove a forty-horse hitch and had

The Africa, sometimes called the India or Hippo wagon, was built for Spellman Motorized Circus in 1919. Later used by other circuses, was destroyed by fire in 1940.

The Ben Wallace bandwagon shown at Peru, Indiana, winter quarters in 1907.

them four abreast. Two horses were on each side of the wagon pole, with two pairs in front on the body pole. The thirty-two others were held in line with traces and reins, but they never pulled any of the load.

Posey had reins in each hand — ten of them — and the lead horses were eighty feet from his seat on the wagon. One man worked the wheel brakes while another helped with the lines.

Circuses used horses of different colors effectively, especially in street parades. There might be teams of all blacks, all whites, or bays, perhaps hitched checkerboard style. The most beautiful and spirited of each color and breed were ridden or driven separately. Most circus horses were geldings.

Ponies, mules, zebras, camels, oxen, and elephants also drew parade wagons. Larger circuses paraded elephants, camels, and zebras in groups, elephants marching trunk to tail.

There were wagons for all the wild animals, from aardvarks to hippopotamuses to zebras, including birds, monkeys, and reptiles. It was common practice to have snake dens with large plate glass windows where women could be seen handling the squirming reptiles as the parade went by.

Cage wagons bore elaborate designs and painted wood panels called sky boards that folded down from above when not in use. Some had carved columns or life-size figures on each corner. Most had plaques or signs with names of animals they contained, for easy identification.

Circuses used all sizes and types of wagons, from elongated affairs for hauling tent poles to miniatures drawn by goats or dogs in street parades and the grand entry. Many were little more than sturdy boxes mounted on wheels and crammed with canvas, stakes, seats, cookhouse equipment, generator and refrigerator units, costumes, and props.

There were wagons and later railroad cars filled with advertising matter and billing crews — wagons for ticket sellers, the manager, and stars of the center ring.

There were special wagons for specific purposes. For example, gilly wagons hauled stakes, hay, and other items. Gilly is a Scotch word for

Hagenbeck-Wallace Circus used this ticket wagon as late as 1934.

assistant or helper, and that's what the gilly wagon was — to help around a lot. It usually was small and drawn by one horse.

Larger circuses had a "pie" car, where personnel could relax and socialize when the work was done. Finally, there were rolling rest rooms, known as donnikers.

The 101 Ranch Wild West had a Longhorn Steer wagon for parades and baggage. It was fourteen feet long, five feet six inches wide, and the main body was three feet six inches deep. The steer rode in an open area atop the wagon body, ten feet long and two feet four inches high. This pen had steel posts on each corner and steel or hemp lines in between, giving everyone a view of the towering animal.

The Ringlings once had a giraffe wagon, drawn by four white horses. The giraffe's head and neck protruded through an opening in the top, giving the animal an opportunity to survey the sidewalk crowds from his lofty perch.

These wagons accomplished just what they were intended to do — attract attention and create an overwhelming urge to see the performance.

CHAPTER FIVE

SINGING WHEELS

FROM THEIR EARLIEST DAYS in America, circuses have gone out into the country looking for business, and thus they have been dependent upon one of the greatest and most useful inventions of mankind — the wheel. But instead of using it simply as something to move upon, they improved on it and beautified it so that the wheel became a most valuable asset and a symbol.

Earliest circuses had light-bodied wagons and large wheels to negotiate the streams and muddy or dusty roads of the time. They depended upon each town they played, not alone for patronage but for supplies for themselves and their animals and often for accommodations.

These could cost both money and time, so they commenced to use tents. They put in the circus cookhouse and even added sleeping accommodations. To transport this heavier equipment the wagons were built stronger and wheels smaller and more rugged.

Even after railroads came into general use and circuses bought long, glistening sleeping cars, stockcars, and miles of flats — always renting engines — they still needed rolling stock to move animals and props from railroad sidings to the show grounds and back.

Wheels were the answer, and no one could forget the street parade. So circus ingenuity made them sparkle and sing, adding sweet, soothing tones to the music of the band, bugles, and calliope.

Circus wagon wheels produced a melody, harmony, and rhythm that can never be duplicated because it is physically impossible to create all contributing factors.

Most of these wheels had twelve to twenty spokes, depending upon size and load to be

Webs jammed between spokes produced distinctive musical notes in circus wheels such as this old steel rimmed type.

moved; spokes often were two or more inches in diameter. On larger wagons, front wheels were smaller than rear so they could turn under the wagon body. On some of the heaviest, largest wagons, wheels were equipped with iron rims up to eight inches wide and one inch thick.

Wheels were made of second-growth hickory or white ash and usually were built by companies other than those who made the wagon bodies.

In the early days, wheels were decorated by designs turned into the spokes and rim by skilled artisans. Later, webs were jammed into grooves between the spokes. That did it. Brilliantly painted in many colors, these gave the effect of sunburst as the wheel turned, and gently rubbed up and down to produce dulcet tones.

The heavy hubs turning on axle shafts and

Some wheels had large hubs, short spokes, but the webs were there, too.

slamming against the shoulders poured out a deep rumble or hollow sound, like the woodwind section of a concert orchestra.

At the same time, wooden webs working up and down in spoke slats created a harmonious whine like violin strings, while iron tires rolling over concrete and cobblestones tied the whole together in coherent sequence, like a fine composition.

The whole, mixed with the rubbing of leather, clatter of hitchings, ring of horses' hooves, and shuffling of elephants' feet resulted in a symphonic production loud enough to be heard and felt from one block to another, yet sweet enough to be enchanting and exhilarating. No other combination of sounds could match it!

Wheels were equipped with brakes in the form of curved wood or metal blocks that pressed against the rim. On steep hills, drag shoes kept wheels and wagons from going out of control. These were made of one-inch steel plate and were dropped in front of the left rear wheel so the wheel would roll into it and skid instead of roll.

A chain fastened to the wagon body from the brake shoe caused it to skid. Once the wagon reached the bottom of the hill, the drag could be released quickly and the wheel freed to roll again.

Wagons, too, were built by skilled workmen of the finest materials to withstand the rough, tough wear of years on the road. Seasoned oak, hickory, and hard maple were favorite woods for bodies, and these had special features not found on other vehicles of the day.

Circus wheels came in all sizes, to meet individual needs and keep the show moving.

This steel rimmed wheel, used many years ago, is undergoing renovation. Note paint scraped off part of sunburst.

Tongues were very wide, to withstand thrusts from each side, and were held in place by single pins so they could be attached or dismantled quickly for greater mobility.

Each wagon bore a number to facilitate loading and unloading, but each had descriptive names such as Whiskers, Dragon, Lion, or Two Hems.

Band wagons, tableaux, and chariots were decorated with ornamented figures of every kind, including Greek gods and goddesses, dancing girls, cupids, horses, elephants, lions, swans, peacocks, eagles, gulls, dragons, reptiles, globes, gargoyles, and intricate scrollwork. One wagon represented the temple of Juno; some were designed in the shape of cottages.

Fine carvings came from the Spanjer brothers of Newark, New Jersey, and Chicago, but there were other skilled artists-carvers who turned out these attractive and durable decorations. White pine was the choice for carving.

Wagons were painted in many colors, with fancy lettering. A liberal amount of gold leaf — not paint — was used. Expensive, yes, but effective and lasting. Many of these grand old wagons, exposed to the elements much of the time, have been around for seventy-five years or more, with an occasional change of paint and repair work.

Among builders who turned out magnificent circus wagons were John Stephenson, Fielding Bros., and Sebastian Wagon Company, all of New York; Thomas Caster Company and Fulton and Walker of Philadelphia.

Also J. S. and E. A. Abbott of Concord, New Hampshire; the Bode Company, Ohlsen Company, and George Schmidt Company, all of Cincinnati, Ohio; Schultz Wagon Company of Dayton, Ohio; Sullivan & Eagles of Peru, Indiana; Coan and Ten Brocke of Chicago; Moeller Bros. of Baraboo, Wisconsin, and Beggs Wagon Company of Kansas City.

Charles Luckey and Leonard Aylesworth built the Two Jesters steam calliope wagon at the Denver, Colorado quarters of the Sells-Floto Circus during the winter of 1920-21. This wagon later appeared in the Hagenbeck-Wallace street parade and still later in the "Old King Cole and Mother Goose" tournament or spectacle, usually shortened to "spec," of Ringling Bros. and Barnum & Bailey Circus.

The tournament or spectacle was a glittering parade of all the performers, human and animal, around the hippodrome track early in the performance.

Doubtless there were many other artistic and energetic craftsmen who built or modified wagons to meet certain needs and specifications.

Most companies which built circus wagons also manufactured omnibuses, brewery wagons and other vehicles for the general trade. These were the main source of revenue, but circus wagons were something special.

Their cost could run from $500 to $2,000, depending upon size and ornateness, and we can be certain that these master craftsmen took extra pride in their work when an order for one or more of these beauties came along.

One of the most massive and costly wagons of modern times was the glass-and-steel compartment built especially for Gargantua the Great, the gorilla bought by John Ringling North in December 1937.

When he went on tour the following season, Gargantua was housed in a glittering compartment built by the Carrier Corporation. Front and rear walls were of three-eighths inch thick steel plate, as was the ceiling. Bars were of seven-eighths inch steel and the floor of oak. Each side was of one-half inch thick plate glass, set double with one-half inch air space between panes.

The center compartment, where Gargantua lived, was twenty feet long by seven wide. Over-all, with frames and braces, the cage wagon measured twenty-five feet two inches long, eight feet three and three-eighths inches wide, and seven feet one and one-eighth inches high.

Dual wheels at each corner were thirty-two inches in diameter and rims eighteen inches. They were equipped with massive rubber tires, and the wagon body rested on leaf springs three inches wide with a fifty-four-inch span.

The tongue measured eleven feet nine inches long and was thirteen inches at its widest point. Doubletrees were forty inches long.

The ceiling held eight 300-watt bulbs, and the cage wagon was painted white with gold stripes and scrolls edged in red. It was rather conservative, so it didn't detract from the big, hairy star.

Gargantua became a tremendous attraction, through a well-planned and executed publicity campaign. He even went to England, by freighter, to appear in the Bertram Mills Circus in London while John Ringling North, the circus president, attended to business. It was reported that Gargantua's cage was too large for the Queen Mary's hatches, hence the trip by freighter.

In 1941 Gargantua the Great was joined by M'Toto, a female gorilla from Havana, Cuba. She occupied quarters identical to his, but hers were

Some of these rugged old wheels weigh 250 pounds or more, to support the great weight of bandwagons.

furnished with a chair, table, and cot. M'Toto had used such items while living in luxury with her owner, Mrs. Marie Hoyt, in Havana. Gargantua had a stout wooden table, where he liked to sit, and a huge rubber tire suspended by a chain.

On Washington's birthday that year, while scores of newsmen and photographers looked on, the two cages were pushed end-to-end and the glass panels removed, but the two gorillas only glared at each other, and the "marriage" was never consumated.

Each cage wagon weighed eleven tons, and the circus said each cost $20,000. Air conditioning, housed in one end, maintained an even temperature of 76 degrees and relative humidity of 50 per cent.

Gargantua the Great traveled with the circus for twelve years and was a real trouper to the end. He was found huddled in a corner of his cage, dead, on November 25, 1949. No circus fan who ever saw him will forget the massive iron, steel, and glass wagon number 97 and the great attraction inside.

CHAPTER SIX

GOLDEN AGE OF WAGONS

THE FIRST AMERICAN CIRCUS to tour England went there for the years 1843 to 1845. Owned by Richard Sands and Lewis B. Lent, it met with considerable success, but it was Seth B. Howes who touched off the ornate circus wagon building spree.

Howes, an experienced showman, went to England with Joseph Cushing as the Howes & Cushing Circus. Business was good, and when Howes came home in the late 1860s he brought several fine parade wagons which his competitors soon set out to match.

One of the largest was the L. B. Lent shell band chariot, which came on the scene around 1870. It measured twenty-two feet long, six feet wide and nine feet six inches high; it was drawn by twenty-four horses. Elaborately carved, it later appeared on the Howes & Cushing show, then in Barnum & Bailey parades in America and Europe.

The Thayer & Noyes Circus, which operated about that time, reportedly had a bandwagon even larger than the Lent chariot. Its measurements were given as twenty-eight feet long and ten feet high.

Among operators who went in strong for colorful wagons were Adam Forepaugh, Cooper & Bailey, John Robinson, Sells Bros., Ringling Bros., Sig. Sautelle and various partners, Gollmar Bros., Walter L. Main, and later Hagenbeck-Wallace and Robbins Bros.

The Forepaugh Lion band chariot was one of the most durable and widely traveled vehicles of its kind. Believed built in the 1870s, it featured carvings of snarling, leaping lions. It had an elevated driver's seat and a still higher awning-type canopy in the rear.

The Lion was on the Buffalo Bill Wild West Show briefly then went to Europe with Barnum & Bailey in 1897. It was on the Forepaugh-Sells Circus in 1910-11 and was declared surplus when that show was taken off the road.

After that, the Lion's history is rather skimpy, but it is believed to have ended its career as part of a calliope wagon, a not unusual occurence for a famous old wagon.

Adam Forepaugh featured a telescoping tableau known as St. George and the Dragon. It bore carved relief figures and scrolls extending eight inches from the sides, while a carving on top depicted St. George astride a white charger slaying the dragon with a spear. The mounting could be lowered into the wagon body for protection when the parade was over.

Ownership of St. George and the Dragon passed to Barnum & Bailey, then to Ringling Bros., where the top carvings were removed, mounted on a small cart, and made into a float. The wagon body had seats built into it and became a band-

Arriving at the lot, the circus sometimes found a sea of mud awaiting it.

Hurry up! Get this seat wagon out or we'll never get set up!

wagon. It was still doing duty when Ringling Bros. and Barnum & Bailey circuses were combined in 1919. Later it went to Christy Bros. and then to Cole Bros. It is now among the more than 125 wagons in the Circus World Museum at Baraboo.

Another notable tab wagon was called the Golden Age of Chivalry. It featured a two-headed dragon with green, scaly skin, glistening white claws, and daggerlike fangs, flaming red tongues, and nostrils breathing fire. A maiden sat on the dragon's back, with a knight templar on each side, while six or eight dappled gray Percherons pulled the wagon.

Bell wagons appeared on the scene from time

Elephants were used to move this Al G. Barnes-Sells Floto Combined Circus wagon, in 1938.

The electrical department was an integral part of the circus.

to time. From the outset they seem to have had too much competition from brass bands and calliopes, but they were really something special.

Gollmar Bros. had a Swiss bell wagon around 1890, ten feet long, five feet wide, and five high on the box — six feet including the sky board. It was played by clarion handles mounted on a console; a pull and release of the handle would cause a hammer to strike the bell.

In 1891 the Ringlings commissioned a bell wagon that topped them all. It was what their press agents called "the colossal cathedral chimes of Moscow's Kremlin Tower."

They claimed it offered "continuous carillons of tremendous tones from tons upon tons of sweet-toned bells — the largest, grandest, heaviest chimes ever heard in America; the Musical Bells of Moscow."

Commonly known as The Bell Wagon, it remained with the show for many years, appearing in the spec of 1948 on rubber tires! Incidentally, the bells were cast in America, not Russia.

Spanjer Bros. of Newark and Chicago made scrolls, figures, and raised letters for many parade wagons. Other fine carvings came from the Milwaukee Ornamental Woodcarving Co. in that city, notably on Ringling wagons.

There were others — real artists in wood — and carvings were readily available of such things as peacocks, dolphins, lions, bears, elephants, and reptiles; mermaids, cupids, gargoyles, and heroic figures to adorn sides, corners, and ends of parade wagons of all sizes.

The Columbia bandwagon, on the Ringling show, was elaborately carved and bore figures of six females on each side, plus an eagle above with an American flag in its talons. The wagon was painted gold and white.

The Ringlings also had wagons representing America, Africa, Asia, and Europe, the United States and Russia. Once they had a tableau wagon with high sky boards and wheel guards, representing Germany.

Mud, mud everywhere, but the show must go on

Hub deep in mud was the fate of this wagon, in Ringling Bros. and Barnum & Bailey Circus.

Barnum & Bailey featured a Spain wagon in 1910, and Robbins Bros. at one time or another had tab wagons representing China, Belgium, and Russia.

Parade wagons usually had plush-lined canvas covers to protect the finish and contents from the elements. Circus personnel knew from experience and by instinct how to meet every challenge.

Merle Evans, bandleader on the Ringling-Barnum show for fifty years, remembers that when it looked like rain, musicians took along raincoats. If it didn't rain during parade, the band used upturned tin buckets for drums, "and they worked out very well."

What's this? Dressage plumes on horses, and a work wagon.

It takes rugged equipment to drive and pull tent stakes

Business was good! Now for the tear down.

Long before mobile homes came into general favor, circus folk lived in wagons. Some shows even had what they called "hospitality rooms," where they entertained specific guests.

When James A. Bailey brought his circus home from Europe in the fall of 1902, he found that the Ringlings had grown both in size and reputation during the five years he had been away. Bailey decided to do something about it.

He contracted with the Sebastian Wagon Company for thirteen parade wagons and floats,

Line up to test water pressure. Ready, Aim!

with carvings by Spanjer Bros., to be used in his triumphal street parade of 1903.

No more eye-popping exhibition ever moved down the streets of any city. This gigantic procession included three great bandwagons — Two Hemispheres, Forepaugh Lion, and L. B. Lent Band Chariot — all elegantly carved, beautifully decorated, and crammed with musicians.

Some say the Five Graces was there, too, and it may have been, for it had just toured Europe with Barnum & Bailey.

Fire away! And all in perfect working order.

These fine wagons (either three or four), combined with gorgeous fairy-tale floats and hundreds of other attractions, made this one of the largest and most spectacular circus parades ever seen anywhere.

The Barnum & Bailey opening spec that year was called "Cleopatra," and it featured magnificent scenery with a cast of 1,250.

A discarded Ringling Bros. and Barnum & Bailey work wagon down among the sheltering palms in Florida.

CHAPTER SEVEN

USEFUL AND ORNAMENTAL

IN THE EARLY YEARS, some circuses rented wagons from builders and dealers or acquired them from other circuses. When the Ringlings started their circus in 1884 they owned only two wagons and rented five.

In his book, *Circus Parades*, Charles P. ("Chappy") Fox tells about the first Ringling bandwagon, built by their cousins, the Moellers, from rough sketches in their wagon shop at Baraboo.

Fox quotes Henry Moeller as saying they took the gear from an old dray, built a fourteen-foot body onto it, and installed seat planks. The body was three and one-half feet high, with a door at the back for loading.

Mirrors set into the sides were tin instead of glass, with wood carvings of eagles. The body was painted red — Ringling red, of course — with moldings and eagles a rich yellow to look like gold.

John Hamilton, the Ringlings' first boss hostler, drove four white horses as a team, and between towns the band rode in this vehicle. First used in the 1885 season, it became the number two bandwagon when the Ringlings went on rails in 1890.

Tab wagons could be roughly divided into three types — those bearing carvings of the insignia of nations; those with paintings of fairy tales, wild animals and Biblical scenes on the sides; and those designed to carry clowns, acrobats, jugglers, and other performers on top.

Many of these gaudy old wagons moved from one circus to another as fortune dictated, or passed from the scene virtually unnoticed, so it is impossible to trace their histories.

Wagon builders went out of business when automobiles replaced buggies and wagons, and many records were lost when they closed shop. Some circus wagons were lost in fires, others splintered in wrecks or were consigned to the junkyard when their owners left the road.

Circus wagons were prime subjects for photographers, but picture-taking did not become

Hagenbeck-Wallace calliope wagon, with horses all dressed up and ready to go.

Sleeping Beauty never made spec at this stand!

But this candy float did make it

popular until early in this century; even then results generally were of mediocre quality, only in black and white, and few negatives were preserved.

It is regrettable that color photography did not come into vogue until recently; it could have captured those magnificent wagons and chariots in all their glory.

Fortunately some of these grand old vehicles have been preserved in museums throughout the country — restored to their original beauty through the cooperation of artists, wood-carvers, historians, and circus buffs. These cherished relics of a bygone era, plus a generous amount of colored posters, artist's sketches, and old photographs still in the hands of museums and private collectors, give a fair and most enlightening pic-

Carl Hagenbeck Greater Trained Animal Shows used this carved, open, double den cage wagon in 1905-06.

This Ringling Bros. and Barnum & Bailey Circus tableau wagon was built for the 50th anniversary and was pulled by ponies.

Elaborate carvings and grotesque figures featured this China tab wagon.

This old wagon was called the India Elephant tab wagon.

*This tableau wagon bore the name of Russia, with appropiate
wood carvings.*

Called the King's Royal Chariot, this tab wagon featured a throne.

This wagon was the Egypt or Cleopatra tableau in the Barnum & Bailey Circus.

ture of the wagons and the roles they played in the American circus.

Truly they were the very heart and soul of the circus parade and vital to the entire operation. Ornamental yet sturdy and durable, they provided needed storage space on the grounds and transportation between towns for both equipment and personnel.

Bands often rode in them from one stand to the next — else they were crammed with horse collars, harness, lines, and other gear. Big circuses had special chariots and floats used only in the parade and grand entry, but these were the exception. Nearly every item on the lot was put to maximum use.

All wagons and other circus equipment were

Ringling Bros. and Barnum & Bailey Circus used this animal transfer cage wagon to move animals from one cage to another.

*This tab wagon, called Funny Folks, was built especially for
clowns, even to the carvings.*

*This Barnum, Bailey & Hutchinson cage wagon had tab cover-
ing but there were bars behind it, and animals inside.*

Miller & Arlington 101 Ranch Real Wild West featured these wagons, some with live animals on top, during the parade.

Miller & Arlington 101 Ranch Real Wild West featured these wagons, some with live animals on top, during the parade.

painted to start each new season. Some featured Biblical and pastoral scenes, seascapes, and historical events; others bore portraits of the circus owner or owners, in full color.

Carvings represented globes, birds, and animals or depicted Cornelia and her Jewels, the Landing of Columbus, Pocahontas and Captain John Smith, and other incidents based on fact or legend.

Several wagons came from abroad, some as late as the 1960s when the Circus World Museum at Baraboo added to its large collection by acquiring six or eight once used by the Fossett Circus in England. A few of these were seen in the Schlitz Fourth of July parade in Milwaukee in the early 1970s.

Barnum & Bailey Circus featured pony fairy tale floats in the 1886-88 seasons. This is Sinbad the Sailor.

Bluebeard was another pony fairy tale float. Note the plain, thin wheels without sunburst.

This Santa Claus pony fairy tale float was used by Barnum & Bailey in 1883.

The last bandwagon to be built in this country (up to 1977) is a white and gold beauty twenty-two feet long and thirteen feet high. Designed by Russell Zimmerman of Milwaukee, the chassis was built by the Wilbur Deppe Co. of Baraboo, with wood carvings by William Thallmayer of Waukesha, Wisconsin.

This wagon was built for the Schlitz Brewing Co. and appeared in the 1973 parade drawn by forty horses, with Dick Sparrow the driver.

Three of the most elegantly carved and beautifully decorated circus wagons ever seen in America were the Five Graces, the Swan, and the Columbus-John Smith, better known as the Pawnee Bill. One of the largest ever built and used as a bandwagon on several shows was the Two Hemispheres, affectionatley called the Two Hems.

These four are the favorites of connoisseurs and circus fans everywhere. Their admirers never tire of visiting, studying, and photographing these splendid examples of the wood-carver's patience, talents, and skill, and the almost forgotten art of wagon building.

CHAPTER EIGHT

THREE OF A KIND

REGARDED AS ONE of the most elegant and massive bandwagons ever constructed is the Pawnee Bill Wild West, preserved with scores of others in the Circus World Museum at Baraboo, operated by the Wisconsin State Historical Society.

The Sebastian Manufacturing Company became the third and last major New York wagon builder and in 1904 delivered the Columbus-John Smith bandwagon to the Pawnee Bill (Gordon W. Lillie) Wild West Show. It was twenty-two feet long and eight feet high.

This wagon was unique in that its carvings depicted different scenes on opposite sides. One showed Columbus and half a dozen others, complete with robes, flags, and swords, landing in the New World. The other featured Captain John Smith just at the moment Pocahontas stepped in to save him from being beheaded by the Indians.

A likeness of Lillie appeared on the sky boards in shell-like frames, with scrollwork extending the length of the boards. Fine scrollwork surrounded the main carvings, and American flags adorned each corner. Carved buffalo heads on each complemented the red, white, and blue of the flags.

All four wheels were identical in size, with sixteen spokes and sunburst panels.

When the Pawnee Bill left the scene in 1913, the wagon went to the Mighty Haag Railroad Show. Its final tour of duty was with the 101 Ranch Wild West. The Bill Hames family of Fort Worth, Texas, donated this fine wagon to the Circus World Museum.

One of the very richly carved and most ornamental of all bandwagons is the Swan, built in Baraboo in 1905 by the Moeller brothers for their cousins, the Ringlings.

Two large swan figures adorn the sides over the front wheels. Carvings also include angels, cupids, birds, and fish on a churning sea. An angelic figure is touching a swan's wing; another

In early days, the Two Hemispheres was painted white and gold.
Later it was red and gold, as it is today.

A pony-sized version of St. George and the Dragon. Later this
was embellished to full size.

The Peter Peter Pumkin Eater parade wagon was used for storage when not on parade. It was a full-size ruggedly-built wagon.

is clutching the harpist's arm who, incidentally, is riding two sea serpents.

An eagle with wings spread adorns the center, and another bird soars in from the horizon. The sea is blue, the background white; exquisite scrollwork frames the entire body. A carved and gilded canopy rises above the rear section. Sunburst wheels with sixteen spokes support the wagon.

The Swan appeared in the Ringling Bros. Circus parade for a few seasons, then went to the Forepaugh-Sells Circus under the same ownership. From there it went to Barnum & Bailey, then to Christy Bros., and finally to Ken Maynard's Diamond K Ranch Wild West and Circus, which operated briefly in 1936.

The Swan was on display at Disneyland in California for some time and was presented to the Circus World Museum by Walt Disney Studios.

We now come to the Five Graces, reputedly the oldest parade wagon still in existence. Built in 1878 by Fielding Bros. of New York for Adam Forepaugh, the Five Graces is a grand reminder of the "glory days" of the American circus.

The Three Graces in Greek mythology were three sisters goddesses named Aglaia, Euphrosyne, and Thalia, who dispensed charm and beauty — but three evidently weren't enough for circus purposes.

Forepaugh's graces were said to represent education, law, peace, religion, and victory, which raises a most interesting question. Were

The Five Graces bandwagon was a popular parade feature, and is reported to be the oldest of its kind still in existence, built in 1878.

The Lion and mirror bandwagon has appeared in the Fourth of July parade in Milwaukee, with Bandmaster Merle Evans aboard.

those designations meant for the Five Graces or
for the five figures on the Howes' Great London
Globe Tableau?

Richard E. Conover, who died a few years ago,
was an authority on circus wagons and wrote
extensively about them. He stated that the
graces on the side of the wagon illustrated "religion, education, law, victory, and peace," and he
compared the Five Graces wagon and Howes'
Globe Tableau in these words:

"The similarity between the Five Graces and
the Howes' Globe Tableau is so confusingly close,
even though the two wagons were made on opposite sides of the Atlantic and one built seven

*This sturdy old bandwagon bore the name Great Britain and
featured great carved lions above scrollwork.*

The great telescoping wagon used on the Fossett Circus in England and brought to this country in the 1960s. It is now on display in the Circus World Museum at Baraboo, Wis.

years later than the other, that only by illustrating them side by side will the difference be apparent to the careless comparator."

The major perceptible differences, he noted, are in the shape of the large irregular mirrors and in the features of the five ladies that grace the panels.

Originally called the "Gem Bossed Car of Freedom," the five graces were "surmounted by the allegorical representation of the Goddess of Liberty," the goddess being the show girl riding in a chair atop the globe.

John H. Hurdle, curator of the Ringling Museum of the Circus and a former president of the Circus Fans Association of America, believes the five graces were meant for Howes' Great London Globe Tableau.

"Looking at pictures of this wagon through a magnifying glass," Hurdle noted, "it is easy to see that the figures are in quite different positions from those on the Graces. Whether they are holding anything or not is difficult to determine.

"But looking at the Graces, it seems obvious to me that the figures are representing the four seasons, for the one on the left is holding a bunch of flowers (spring). Moving to the right, the next is holding what appears to be fruit (summer).

"The center figure holding the sword represents Columbia, or this country. Moving again to the right, the figure is holding both a scythe and a bundle of wheat (fall and harvest time).

"And the next one is the only one with shoes, a cloak with a cowl, and is holding what looks like a little pot of fire in the left hand while she warms her right over it — obviously winter.

"These features are so strong and distinctive that I believe they are symbolically representing the fruits and productivity of this country. Other than the visual symbolism I have no proof of the theory but feel strongly about it."

Hurdle adds that some fans still insist they are the Three Graces of Greek mythology and that old Forepaugh said three weren't enough and ordered two more — but he thinks this is absurd.

Evidence is strongly in favor of Hurdle, who not only is an authority on circuses but has the Five Graces wagon right in his own museum.

The Globe remained atop the Gem Bossed Car of Freedom at least until 1883 and possibly longer. It may have been removed and the name Five Graces applied following the railroad wreck the Forepaugh Circus had near Downington, Pennsylvania, enroute to winter quarters in Philadelphia at the close of the 1885 season.

According to Conover, the wagon was in that wreck and reports of the time said it was so badly damaged it would never be seen again. The same was said of others, but the following spring the Five Graces was the number one bandwagon in the Forepaugh parade. It stayed there for nine seasons, until Bailey took the show off the road.

By now the globe had been removed and placed on another wagon body, surrounded by carved figures of men, women, and lions.

The Five Graces was in the Barnum & Bailey parades of 1897, drawn by forty horses with Jake Posey handling the reins for this ten-ton band-wagon. Barnum & Bailey went to England that fall and took the Five Graces there.

Moving to the continent in 1900, the circus gave its last street parade on European soil in October, except for one special occasion in France in 1902.

Barnum & Bailey returned home in November of that year, and the Five Graces was shoved into second place by a great new and larger bandwagon — the Two Hemispheres.

When Barnum & Bailey discontinued street parades in 1905, the Five Graces went into temporary retirement. It was not seen again until 1910 and 1911, when it appeared on the Forepaugh-Sells Circus, then owned by Ringling Bros.

Conover reported that the Five Graces was rebuilt in the winter of 1911-12 by Moeller Bros. at a total cost of $319.83. When the Ringling Bros. and Barnum & Bailey Combined Circus discontinued parades in 1920, the Five Graces went off the road again and did not make another appearance for fourteen years.

It apparently was in Bridgeport, Connecticut, most of that time, but in the spring of 1934 it joined the Hagenbeck-Wallace Circus in Peru, Indiana, for the 1935 season.

Records indicate it was off the road in 1936, but it appeared briefly the next year on Hagenbeck-Wallace, which at that time was under lease to Howard Y. Bary.

"Jake Posey was also there as boss hostler and, as he related it, Bary was ambitious to revive the forty-horse hitch; in fact, Bary wanted to do it one better and add four more horses," Conover wrote. "Somehow enough leather was

Ringling Bros. Circus featured a bell wagon once painted white and gold, later changed to red and gold.

The United States bandwagon included flags and figures on each side, with benches for the band members on top.

gathered to put it together, but one tug was enough to tear it apart.

"So ended the first and only forty-four-horse hitch ever assembled, and the Graces was returned to the Peru winter quarters."

Fortunately, in the wartime scrap drives of 1941 and 1942 the Five Graces was overlooked, accidentally or on purpose. Many other wagons that had outlived their usefulness or needed repair became splinters and scrap iron.

The Bode Wagon Works of Cincinnati built sixteen tableaux for the United States Motorized Circus. The bodies were mounted on trucks and each represented a nation — the Un-

The Pawnee Bill tableau wagon was one of the most elaborately carved of them all. This side shows Columbus landing in the new world; the other side features Captain John Smith and Pocahontas.

Zack Terrell presented the Two Hemispheres bandwagon to Col. B. J. Palmer of Davenport, Iowa, in 1944. Pictured above are Palmer, Terrell, Mrs. Estraleta Terrell and Noyelles Burkhart.

ited States, Great Britain, Belgium, France, and others.

Because of World War I, the wagon representing Germany never was completed, according to some sources, and the U.S. Motorized Circus never made it. Some of the sides of the tableau wagons later appeared on the Robbins Bros. Circus and still later on Cole Bros.

The Five Graces spent most of World War II in winter quarters at Peru but in April 1944 joined five other historic old wagons on something of a sentimental journey from Indiana to Ringling Bros. and Barnum & Bailey Circus winter quarters at Sarasota.

The fine old wagon has been in Florida ever

since, except for the 1945 season when it was in the Ringling-Barnum spec. Shortly afterward it went on display in the Ringling Museum of the Circus, operated by the State of Florida as part of the Ringling Museums Complex.

There it's a near neighbor of another grand old bandwagon that deserves special attention — the Two Hemispheres.

The eastern side of the Two Hemispheres featured England, France, Spain, Russia, Belgium and Italy.

CHAPTER NINE

A WHOPPING WAGON

MUCH HAS BEEN WRITTEN about the goliath of circus wagons, the Two Hemispheres — some of it pure fiction wearing the cloak of fact. It's a shame, too, because the famous old Two Hems was, and still is, one of the largest ever put on the road and a splendid example of fine wagon building and wood carving. Surely the truth will suffice.

It was designed and built in 1902 — not 1896 as some reports have it, and certainly not for P. T. Barnum, who died in 1891. It was one of the wagons and floats built for the Barnum & Bailey Circus parade in the 1903 season.

Designed by Harry Ogden of the Strobridge Lithographic Co. of Cincinnati, it was built by the Sebastian Wagon Co. of New York, with wood carvings supplied by the Spanjer Bros. in Newark.

The wagon measures twenty-eight feet in length, seven feet eleven inches wide at the center, and ten feet six inches high. Wheels in front are forty-two inches in diameter, the rear wheels forty-eight inches. They are fitted with steel rims.

It has been proclaimed the largest parade

wagon ever built. Some authorities dispute this, pointing out that a thing called the Chariot of India, brought to this country from Europe in the 1860s, was reported to be thirty-five feet long.

Anyway, the Two Hemispheres was loaded with carved medallions representing nations of the Eastern and Western hemispheres, and all were beautifully executed.

On the Eastern Hemisphere side were seals of Great Britain, France, Russia, Germany, Austria, and Italy. During World War I the medallion representing Germany was replaced by one for Belgium, and Austria was changed to Spain.

The Western Hemisphere was represented by Chile, Argentina, Brazil, Mexico, Canada, and

The western side had carved medallions of Chile, Argentina,
Brazil, Mexico, Canada and the United States.

Front and rear of the Two Hemispheres bandwagon were elaborately carved, too. This view shows the rear carvings.

the United States. The name Barnum & Bailey was above the globe representing the Eastern Hemisphere and Ringling Bros. above the globe on the western side.

Huge carved letters "B" were inside whorls over the wheels on both sides. Apparently no one was around to carve the letter "R" for Ringling, or no one thought of it. Carvings of wild animals supported large ovals depicting the hemispheres.

Because it was more than twenty feet long, the mammoth band wagon was designated 142 and 143 for loading and unloading, but it was commonly known among workmen on the lot and by circus buffs as the Two Hems or simply The Hem.

In the 1903 and 1904 street parades the wagon was drawn by a forty-horse hitch, but in 1905 and thereafter hitches of twelve and twenty-four horses were used. Ten horses pulled it in the Ringling Bros. and Barnum & Bailey parades in 1919 and 1920.

Some reports had Jake Posey, the famous forty-horse driver, on this wagon in Europe, but Jake denied it. He was there with the Buffalo Bill Circus, then owned by Barnum & Bailey, from 1903 to 1906, but the Two Hems was not. Jake has been quoted by authoritative sources as saying he never saw the wagon.

One report said Posey gave the wagon to Fred Buchanan, who then operated the Robbins Bros. Circus. Posey might have arranged for the wagon to go to Buchanan, but we'll go along with his statement that he never saw it.

*Mrs. Ike Rose and the famous Rose Midgets contrast with the
front of the towering Two Hemispheres.*

When Barnum & Bailey toured Europe, the
parade wagons included the gorgeous Five
Graces, Van Amburgh & Co.'s Great Golden
Chariot, and L. B. Lent's Fielding Chariot, a
twenty-two foot-long, shell-type wagon that first
appeared on Lent's New York Circus in 1870.

The Two Hemispheres was added when Barnum & Bailey came home from Europe, and the
Van Amburgh band chariot was replaced by the

Forepaugh Lion band chariot, one of the most durable ever to appear in a circus parade.

Believed to have been built some time between 1866 and 1870, the Lion was around for at least sixty-five years and was rolling much of that time. It featured great carved lions on all four corners, and roaring lions centering whorled carvings above the rear wheels. Of course front and rear panels bore fine carvings, too, as did all parade wagons of the time.

The Lion went from Adam Forepaugh to Barnum & Bailey, to Ringling Bros., to Fred Buchanan, to William P. Hall, and finally back to Buchanan, who sent out the Robbins Bros. Circus in 1924.

It probably had more owners and traveled with more circuses than any other wagon in America. Sides of the Lion ended up on Buchanan's calliope wagon, a not unusual end for such colorful carvings.

Finally the old Lion calliope wagon was consigned to the Buchanan barnyard at Granger, Iowa, about 1927 and was joined there a few years later by the Two Hemispheres!

When the Ringling Bros. and Barnum & Bailey properties were consolidated to open the 1919 season, Charles Ringling hired Merle Evans, a twenty-five-year-old cornet player lately of the Buffalo Bill Wild West Show, as bandleader for the big one. Merle and his band rode in the Two Hemispheres in the 1919 and 1920 parades.

"We used ladders to get into the wagon," Merle recalled recently, "one in front and one in back. When the last man climbed in, we'd pull the ladders up. When we were ready to unload, we'd drop them and climb down. Usually all they carried in this big old wagon was harness and horse collars.

"Ten horses pulled it in parade, and it was a good wagon to ride — sturdy and never used for anything except the parade. They said it weighed five tons, and I believe it.

"I remember once when we were coming off Boston Common, the wagon ran away on a steep hill. We were hanging on the side, and I thought sure it would go over when we turned into

A tractor moved the Two Hemispheres on grounds of the Palmer School of Chiropractic at Davenport, Iowa.

Boyleston Street. That wagon was a long one, and it stayed side up, but we never thought it would. We were a scared bunch of musicians.

"Four buglers led the parade, and the sideshow band rode in the Five Graces with eight horses pulling it. This was a nice wagon, but nothing like the Hemisphere.

"On the show at that time we had the big show band, sideshow band, mounted band, clown and ticket sellers' bands, a steam calliope, and sixteen camels pulling a Deagan Unifone.

"The parade had plenty of music, and it was really something. We made parade in 1919 and 1920, and that was it."

After the big show discontinued street parades, the Two Hemispheres went to winter quarters in Bridgeport. It next appeared on the Robbins Bros. Circus, operated by Fred Buchanan from 1924 through 1930.

By this time the depression had spread like a fog, and rather than haul this big, bulky wagon from city to city, Buchanan placed it in quarters at Granger, to join the Lion calliope and other properties.

Next the Two Hemispheres was given to the Circus Fans Association of Iowa, which in turn presented it to the president, Jacob Wagner of Des Moines, an enthusiastic circus fan. The story is that Wagner in his will provided that it go to the Cole Bros. Circus, then operated and owned by Zack Terrell and Jess Adkins.

It was paraded a few times but was so large and difficult to maneuver it became a liability. Besides creating problems of loading and unloading, it crumbled city streets between the runs and the lot.

While the Cole Bros. Circus was at the Iowa State Fairgrounds in Des Moines, it was decided to leave the big, cumbersome "white elephant" there. The wagon was placed alongside an exhibit building and covered with canvas for protection. This covering bore the initials RB&BB on all four sides and the wagon's numbers, 142-143.

In the meantime Jess Adkins passed away and Zack Terrell became sole owner of Cole Bros. The Two Hems was still in the open, still covered with canvas in the early 1940s when the show played Davenport, Iowa.

There into the picture came a circus fan named Colonel B. J. Palmer, operator of a chiropractic school in that city, who had as his guests that day Zack Terrell and his wife, Estraleta. The subject of the big, old bandwagon came up, and Zack reportedly offered it to Palmer if he would restore it and house it in a suitable building.

The wagon arrived in Davenport from Des Moines aboard a low-boy truck and went into an exhibition building at the Mississippi Valley Fairgrounds.

Palmer hired two wood-carvers to rebuild the wagon, and they replaced all wood that had fallen to dry rot. Most of the wagon was disassembled and the paint burned and sanded off.

It was reassembled and painted Ringling red, trimmed in gold. This work was done by Ken Hall, a Davenport artist and painter. Palmer reportedly spent $8,500 for gold leaf to be applied to the wagon, and he inspected the work frequently.

Early in World War II the wagon was used in parades to head up war bond drives. It was drawn by ten- and twelve-horse teams of Belgians. If horses were not available, tractors did the job.

When the Ringling Bros. and Barnum & Bailey Circus played Davenport on September 11, 1944, the Two Hemispheres was moved to the municipal stadium for the day. Merle Evans and his band were photographed in the wagon for old times' sake.

Two years later Palmer built a concrete block building near his Palmer School of Chiropractic, and the bandwagon went on display there, along with sunburst wheels and other circus material the chiropractor had collected.

A large multicolored neon sign atop the building blazed each evening. It read, "Home of the Greatest Bandwagon on Earth."

The Two Hems made a few outside appearances, and whenever circuses played Davenport, Palmer invited his show business friends to see it. A booklet about the building and its contents contained many photographs.

Business apparently wasn't too brisk, because Palmer said he tried to give the wagon away. He offered it to museums in Chicago, Detroit, and Washington, but none had room for it.

A promoter as well as circus buff, Palmer then sent the wagon, along with some two dozen sunburst wheels and other circus material, to Sarasota, Florida, where he had an interest in a project called the Circus Hall of Fame, which was and still is privately owned.

It was a day's work just to get the Two Hems ready for the trip and load it onto a flatcar. It was planned to chock the wheels and let it ride, but railroad men said that wouldn't do because of the great weight. So the wheels were removed, and the wagon rested on axles and bed. It was anchored with cables, and a new piece of canvas, bought especially for the journey, protected it from the weather.

The Two Hems rode the Rock Island Railroad to Chicago, the Illinois Central to Birmingham, Alabama, and the Atlantic Coast Line (now the Seaboard Coast Line) to Sarasota. There the Two Hemispheres sits like a queen in the great glassed-in lobby of the Circus Hall of Fame, in

Two Hemispheres bandwagon being loaded from a flatbed truck to a train at Davenport, Iowa, for the trip to Florida.

Loaded aboard the flat car, the Two Hemispheres was too top-heavy to make the trip.

This photograph shows wheels being removed, so the Two
Hemispheres would sit flat on the flat car.

glittering red and gold. (At one time it was painted white and gold.)

It has made only one outside appearance, and this was for a television program. Workmen had to remove the entire plate glass side of the building to get it out.

In the courtyard beyond are many other wagons, dens, and cages, plus a score or more sunburst wheels, some weighing 250 pounds or more. Circus greats are honored in surrounding hallways and alcoves.

The Two Hems is plainly visible from U.S. 41, only a few hundred yards north of the state-owned and operated Ringling Museums complex.

Here is the John Ringling mansion, the John and Mable Ringling Museum of Art containing one of the finest collections of Rubens in the world, the Asolo Theater brought piece by piece from Italy, and the Museum of the Circus, home of the Five Graces, Two Jesters, and other circus wagons and tableaux, plus a valuable display of circus models, posters, and photographs.

The strangest part of the Two Hemispheres chronicle is that nowhere in its many years of moving from one circus to another, one owner to another, one station to another, is there a single mention of money. Love for the circus and its traditions, and the urge to preserve this and many another fine old wagon or cage, protected and governed them. Generous hearts and skilled hands rescued them from junkyards, restored them to their original beauty, and preserved them for all to see and enjoy as authentic links to yesteryear.

CHAPTER TEN

CIRCUSES LIVE ON

MANY OF THE fine old circus wagons, and even complete shows, of another era are with us today — in miniature — through efforts of model builders, a dedicated group of energetic men and women who spend their spare time re-creating these renowned relics.

"Our people may not have been born in a circus backyard or on a train, or even have traveled with a show, but they love the circus so much and want one so badly they build their own," said Freddie Daw, former president of the Circus Model Builders, Inc.

Organized forty years ago, they now have nearly 2,000 active members in forty-eight "rings" throughout the United States and Canada, with others all over the world. Members must be sixteen years of age, but there are junior members and a ladies auxiliary.

There are five geographical districts called "lots," and to attend one of these gatherings is likely to bring on "circus fever."

Watching these skilled artisans set up and operate their exhibits at biennial conventions in such cities as Allentown, Pennsylvania (1970), Brewer, Maine (1972), Indiana, Pennsylvania

(1974), and Springfield, Ohio (1976) is an absorbing and enlightening experience.

Productions may represent the largest circus in the world or the smallest — perhaps one in between. It may have been famous for many years or might have lasted a single season.

Most start with one wagon, built to scale one-eighth inch, one-quarter, one-half or even an inch. If a member lives on a farm, with plenty of room, he may build a full-sized wagon.

Add more wagons, horses, elephants, camels,

Monkey Wagon, one-eighth scale – James Parker, Key West, Florida.

Pony Fairy Tale Floats, one-fourth scale (A) Cinderella and Prince Charming; (B) Little Red Riding Hood and the Wolf; (C) Old Mother Goose; (D) The Old Woman in a Shoe – By Bettie Daw, Coral Gables, Florida.

and other animals; put in cages, flats, sleepers, tents, and midway; add performers and many workingmen; throw in a cookhouse; work in props and thousands of spectators — and there's your circus!

The completed models, with all the colors and trappings, are things of exquisite beauty. Some are animated, so that when tiny lights blink on in the big top, the band plays, the grand entry is underway, and music of a sort comes from the smoking, steaming calliope little larger than a pack of cigarettes!

Most buy their wagons, sides, and end pieces already carved, get wheels and running gear from dealers, and assemble and paint their own. One builder may specialize in wheels, another in springs and tongues, and a third in figurines.

Some supply light canvas for tents of all sizes, from a saucer to a bedspread. These come complete with tent poles, stakes, and nylon lines.

Painting is a painstaking chore, done with tiny brushes of two hairs or more. Everything is

Sig Sautelle Pony Bandwagon, one-fourth scale – Arthur Thompson, Niles Illinois.

Parade and Work Wagons, one-fourth scale. (A) Display or spec wagon; (B) Bell or Chime wagon; (C) Cookhouse wagon – Dr. Robert Immel, Massillon, Ohio.

covered with special paint, down to the elephant's toenails.

Clowns and other performers are painted in authentic colors; eyes of center ring stars will not only be properly colored but shaded underneath! Roustabouts will be in proper uniforms, and aerialists perform on lines no larger than a spider's web.

Watch one of these artists working at assembling the parts of a wagon or railroad car. Likely as not, he will be chewing gum rapidly and will pause a moment to lay the wad aside.

When it hardens a bit, he will shape it into a

Original calliope wagon, built from scatch, one-fourth scale – H. T. Dreyfus, Houston, Texas.

Cage wagon and band wagons, one-fourth scale. (A) Gargantua cage wagon; (B) Pawnee Bill (1) and Two Hemispheres (r); (C) Swan (1) and Five Graces (r) – Bernard G. Corbin, Red Oak, Iowa.

Tab and Cage wagons, one-fourth scale. (A) Scratch-built tab-leau; (B) Scratch-built lion cage wagon – Dr. M. B. Ryckman, St. Thomas, Ontario, Canada.

Parade wagons, one-fourth scale. (A) Cage wagon; (B) Lion and Gladiator tab wagon; (C) Two Jesters calliope wagon – Earl Schmid, Pittsburgh, Pennsylvania.

tub for the elephants' act — or roll it into a ball, apply a drop a red paint and, presto! There's a ball for the seal's nose.

Quantities of paint and glue go into the production, but the doubletrees may be made of matchsticks, and hay may be finely chopped grass.

Members often exchange hints and ideas for improving production, along with photographs and measurements of their favorite wagons, props, and performers.

One builder, insisting on complete authenticity, changed to a pre-1930 model and made all railroad cars of wood because about that time the Interstate Commerce Commission decreed steel coaches as a safety measure.

Lion cage wagon, one inch scale. – Robert B. Clarke, Ocala, Florida.

Knight and Armor bandwagon, one-fourth inch scale. – Carl Helbing, Phoenix, Arizona.

It is estimated that it requires 8,000 to 10,000 hours to build and assemble a complete model circus. Some have spent twenty to thirty years putting together their favorite show of up to 1,000 figures in personnel, up to 100 railroad cars, plus all the animals, wagons, cages, tents, and crowds at a performance.

Many miniature circuses are laid out in basements or attics, but the more affluent may set them up in buildings adjacent to or near their homes. The more sophisticated models are electrified, so that when the owner throws a switch the circus comes to life.

Then we see the crowded midway, the sideshow, menagerie tent, dressing and cook tents. The blacksmith, standing beside his flaming forge, is shoeing a horse. Children are playing and clothes drying on lines in the backyard. On one model there's a barrel the size of a shotgun shell, painted red with the words "no bathing" in white. A tiny figure of a man, nude to the waist, bobs up and down, dripping water!

Teachers have found model-building stimulating and useful in their classrooms, particularly in areas where circuses originated or now maintain winter quarters. It is most helpful in teaching drawing, history, and art.

There are dealers in circus photographs, in model kits, wagons, wheels, springs, seating, blocks for rigging, nuts, bolts, brass tubing, hinges, canvas, lines, and stakes, all to scale. Many advertise their wares in the Little Circus Wagon, official publication of the Circus Model Builders, Inc.

The magazine also prints news of lot and tent gatherings, other items of interest to members and fans, and plans and specifications for all types of equipment from flags to flats.

Two other nationwide organizations, who also have members in other countries, help keep circus memories alive — the Circus Historical Society and the Circus Fans Association. Their magazines — The Bandwagon and The White Tops, respectively — plus a lively quarterly called Southern Sawdust, carry news of interest to circus buffs and authentic accounts of shows and personalities of the past.

But it is the dedicated circus model builder who satisfies his urge to own a circus, who as-

Typical circus model builders display room. Bettie and Freddie Daw, Coral Gables, Fla.

sembles it with infinite skill, patience, and energy, and who brings happy memories to thousands each year by setting up in convention halls, libraries, store windows, and homes.

Here one may see and enjoy in miniature, but accurate in every detail, many of the grand old tented circuses that entertained Americans for two hundred years — surely the greatest outdoor amusement enterprises ever created by man.

BIBLIOGRAPHY

A History of the Circus in America, by George L. Chindahl (Caxton, 1959)

Barnum, by M. R. Werner (1908)

Circus! From Rome to Ringling, by Marian Murray (Appleton-Century-Crofts, 1956)

Circus in America, by Charles Philip Fox and Tom Parkinson (Country Beautiful, 1969)

Circus Parades, by Charles Philip Fox (Century House, 1953)

Gargantua, Circus Star of the Century, by Gene Plowden (Seemann, 1972)

Great Bands in America, by Alberta Powell Graham (Thomas Nelson & Sons, 1951)

Great Days of the Circus, text by Freeman Hubbard (American Heritage, 1962)

John Ringling, by Richard Thomas (Pageant Press, 1960)

Little Circus Wagons, Official publication of the Circus Model Builders.

Merle Evans, Maestro of the Circus, by Gene Plowden (Seemann, 1971)

My Father Owned a Circus, by Robert H. Gollmar (Caxton, 1965)

Struggles and Triumphs, or Forty Years Recollections, by P. T. Barnum (J. B. Burr & Company, 1869)

Struggles and Triumphs, or Forty Years Recollections, by P. T. Barnum (Warren, Johnson & Co., 1873)

The Bandwagon, official publication of the Circus Historical Society.

The Big Top, by Fred Bradna and Hartzell Spence (Simon & Schuster, 1952)

The English Circus, by Ruth Manning-Sanders (Werner Laurie, 1952)

The Fielding Band Chariots, by Richard E. Conover (Privately printed, 1969)

The Life of P. T. Barnum, written by himself (Sampson Low, Son & Co., 1855)

The Ringlings, Wizards of the Circus, by Alvin E. Harlow (Julian Messner, 1951)

The White Tops, official publication of the Circus Fans Association

Those Amazing Ringlings and Their Circus, by Gene Plowden (Caxton, 1967)